A Guide from Domestic Violence To FREEDOM

Nina Hart

Six Hearts
publishing

The first step to getting help is to acknowledge the abuse. Write in this guide and empty your soul. It will point you to a source that will take you to a safe place where you will eventually be Free!

Domestic Violence

According to Wikipedia, domestic violence, also known as domestic abuse, spousal abuse, battering, family violence, and intimate partner violence (IPV), has been broadly defined as a pattern of abusive behaviors by one or both partners in an intimate relationship such as marriage, dating, family, or cohabitation. Domestic violence, so defined, has many forms, including physical aggression (hitting, kicking, biting, shoving, restraining, slapping, throwing objects), or threats thereof; sexual abuse; emotional abuse; controlling or domineering; intimidation; stalking; passive/covert abuse (e.g., neglect); and economic deprivation. Alcohol consumption and mental illness can be co-morbid with abuse, and present additional challenges when present alongside patterns of abuse.

Domestic violence has no regard for gender,
socioeconomic status, ethnicity,
religious preference or age. It can affect anyone.

Text & Cover Design by Huntley Burgher
Published by Six Hearts Publishing
Davie, Florida 33328
www.sixheartspublishing.com

ISBN: 978-0-9845767-6-0
Library of Congress Control Number: 2011919707

Printed in the United States of America

Scripture quotations used in this booklet are from,
The King James Version (KJV) and the New International Version (NIV)
of the Bible

Dedication

For every victim of domestic violence past or present,
this book is dedicated to you... walk in your Freedom

The Purpose

Forgiveness is not about the other person it is about you. It is important for the reader to know that I have completely forgiven my ex-husband. For all I know, he can be a totally new person. God can change anyone as long as they seek Him.

The purpose of this book is not to bash the abuser or men. The purpose is to make people aware of domestic violence and its consequences. The purpose is to bring hope to people in a situation they feel is hopeless. The purpose is for current victims to know that they are not alone, and that other people have gone through similar situations, but now they are free.

If I can successfully walk away from a severely abusive relationship with my six children, then you can do it too. However, it is nothing miraculous that I have done, but God's mercy and grace that has completely turned my situation around.

Acknowledgements

I must first acknowledge my Lord and Savior, Jesus Christ for giving me the outline for one of my DOMESTIC VIOLENCE workshops, which I am now releasing as a book; *'A Guide from Domestic Violence to Freedom.'*

James 1:5 states; *"If any of you lacks wisdom, he should ask God, who gives generously to all without finding fault, and it will be given to him."*

That's what I did when Dr. Cislin Williams recommended me for this workshop, I asked God for wisdom to present this message on domestic violence the way He wanted me to present, not the way I wanted to.

I'd like to give a hearty thanks to all the churches, groups and individuals who invited me to speak on domestic violence here in the States and also in Jamaica. The Lord has already opened up several third world countries where He wants me to take this message in 2012 and going forward. While I wait on the Lord I would like to acknowledge these mighty servants of God for publicly taking a stand against domestic violence, the fact is, many churches are not opened to this teaching. If you are one such individual or church, please find a place in your heart for this message, but for the grace of God, your daughter, mother or sister could be a victim. The message I bring, ultimately gives praise and honor to Jesus Christ for His saving Grace.

To my contingency of supporters living in Jamaica: Rev. Desmond Smith and his beautiful wife Mauva, Ms. Wilma Grandison, Rev. Dr. Maxine White, Sis. Judy Mowatt, Dr. Nsombi Jaja, Rev. Herro Blair, Ian Boyne, Desbert and Julin James, Karl Hart, Vinnette and Kirk Smith along with the hosts of advocates who supported the various events, thank you for the hundreds of emails received from the television and radio interviews, thank you all. Lives were positively impacted, to all my family and friends, I am unable to mention every name, but you know who you are and I am forever grateful. Thank you all and please help me make a change in the lives of victims of domestic violence and their children.

To my sisters at; The Miracle Signs & Wonder Prayer line, the daughters of Zion, thank you Sister Barbara Nelson for inviting me to this 'Anointed,' prayer line. I thank God that this is a platform where women are encouraged to speak up and speak out, pray, cry and just praise God without being criticized or judged. A place where the abused and the free have a voice. Pastor Elaine Bookal, God has a crown awaiting you for your obedience and diligence in intercession. Both you and Pastor Ricky Bookal are champions for the Lord! Mommy Cherry, (my spiritual mother), a committed woman of God who God has called to teach on Forgiveness, thank you for always giving prayers, love and lots of blessings. Sister Vashti Ramnarine, thank you for teaching on the Spirit and the Soul, your gratitude to God for using you despite your past is humbling. Evangelist Geeta, thank God for your boldness to globalize the message of Salvation. May all your needs be met according to Christ's riches in glory. Juliet Waugh of Christians In Action Trade Show, thank you for taking the message of Salvation across this country, Sandy Isaacs, thank you for consistently providing different forums for us to get our messages out. Desmond Hannibal and Michelle Reid, thank you for having a heart for the abused.

Miracle Worship Center, Tamarac Florida; Bishop Dr. Horatio and

Pastor Dr. Winsome Louden, also Sis. Veronica Archibald, thank you for inviting me to speak at the; 'Battered but not Broken,' workshop and to all my sisters and brothers in Christ at Miracle may God bless you all. Thank you Dr. Dennis Grant of the Restoration Center to be among the first churches in South Florida to take a stand with me against domestic violence. To Reverends: Jeff and Loren Terrelonge, thank you for the opportunity to speak at your prayer Luncheon, Pastor Loren, thank you for your vision in helping the abused, may God pour out His blessings on 'Esther's Palace - A Place of Restoration. Sister Trudy Phillips, thanks for making the connection. Bishop Sedroy and Lady Shernet Williams, thank you always for your words of encouragement and for taking a stand against domestic violence. Minister Ingrid Campbell, of Light of The World Christian Center, you and team are doing a great job with the youth. 'From Flawed Vessels to Vessels of Honor.' Bro.Marlon Bolton of Harvest Community Church of God, your Text ministry is a blessing to hundreds, soon to be thousands, thank you for feeding the homeless weekly. Minister Carla Smith, an Intercessor that is being used by Almighty God. Bishop Paul Lyttle and Lady Bridgette Lyttle, thank you for giving me the opportunity to speak at Prayer Breakfast. First Lady Christine Baker and Dr. Kelvin Baker, of 'The Way Fellowship Center,' thank you for helping to heighten the awareness of domestic violence. Pastor Charles Baxter of First Church of God, Fort Lauderdale, thank you for taking a stand against domestic violence. Special thanks to Joseph Jackson, a man after God's own heart. Rev. Dr. Gillian Bishop, thank you for the exposure and the amazing work you are doing on behalf of women. Rev. Jordan Black, thank you for being transparent and for allowing God to use you. Lady Dawn Johnson, anointed to sing for the Lord! To my sister Donna Hart, abused but not broken.

Special acknowledgement to Pastor Shimon Taylor and the leadership of the Deerfield Beach Seventh Day Adventist Church, Sis. Novelette Barrett, a woman who God has blessed with the gift of connecting others, thank you for all you do, along with your dedicated husband

Kenneth to help encourage victims of Domestic Violence. Thanks to the Ft. Lauderdale Seventh Day Adventist Church, for taking an active role in exposing domestic violence, to my friends, Hyacinth and her daughter Ellen Goffe, may God bless and protect you both.

Dr. Cislin Williams, my mentor, a woman of God, completely sold out to the Lord. A servant of God who takes the message of entering into the Holy of Holies to the body of Christ. Apostle Winston Williams, I thank God that you have joined forces with us to help promote the message of 'Freedom from domestic violence,' throughout the churches.

Pastor Vernon Roberts, I thank God that He has given you a repentant heart. Thank God that grace and mercy has stepped in and given you a second chance. I pray that men will be drawn to Christ because of your testimony and they will desire to have the joy that you have experienced in the Lord.

I would like to recognize these organizations and all others that are working globally to eradicate domestic violence from the society. Safespace in Miami Dade, Women in Distress of Broward County and Sheridan House, the latter meets both the physical and spiritual needs of the victims.

To all the individuals who have willingly shared their testimonies with the hope that lives will be changed, I thank you all from the bottom of my heart, may God continue to bless you as you boldly take a stand against domestic violence.

Foreword

I'd rather go through a forest with a guide who has successfully made the journey, rather than a guide who has simply read about the forest but has no experiential knowledge. In Nina's book, *A Guide from Domestic Violence to Freedom,* you will be guided by an experienced and expert guide.

Nina has lived the experience of being an abused wife, as well as seeing her children being abused, physically, emotionally, psychologically and otherwise. Rather than making those experiences mold her into a bitter individual that has developed the victim mentality, she has chosen to facilitate the process of a safe delivery for those who are suffering a similar fate. She has also gone a step beyond guiding the abused victim to teaching others how to be aware of abuse regardless of how subtle it may appear.

There is light at the end of the tunnel. Not everyone who has been a victim of abuse or is presently suffering abuse has to make their exit in a body bag. Through this guide, you will be armed with information that will allow you to experience freedom, and a life after abuse. Those who have not been victimized in this manner will have a better understanding of this malady and be better able to facilitate a process of delivery for victims of domestic abuse. At the end of each section, Nina has provided some thought-provoking questions. Working through each of these sections will help the abused victim to start the process of deliverance, as you yield to the Holy Spirit and allow Him to empty your soul.

In my work as an educator for over twenty-five years, I have witnessed students behaving in ways that I now know indicated the presence of abuse. In those days, I did not have a documentation such as this to help me to better understand and detect domestic violence. With this work in hand, you are better equipped to facilitate a delivery process. The statistics of domestic abuse are staggering and it is time we rise up as individuals, and as a community, hence a nation and set at liberty those that are bound.

Dr. Cislin Williams
Speaker/Teacher/Life-Coach
John Maxwell Team

D – Divine Intervention

According to Wikipedia the definition of Divine Intervention is a miracle caused by God's involvement.

If you were a victim of domestic violence then someone may have come to your rescue. It may have been a brother, cousin, mother, child or even a neighbor. However, something happened to disrupt the plan of the enemy. Many of you might look back on the different incidents in your life and think that it was luck that rescued you. However, it is important for you to understand that it was God who intervened. You see, God has a plan for your life and that was the only reason why He spared you.

Maybe you have questions for God that has not been answered, but I had them too. Often times I would ask God, "Why did you allow my husband to get this close to stabbing me with the knife? Where were you Lord, where were you in all of this?"

The Lord assured me that He allowed my husband's cousin to come at the right time to disrupt the plan of the enemy.

Genesis 50:20 "You intended to harm me, but God intended it for good."

Folks after I got this revelation it humbled me, and I listened to the quiet voice of the Lord taking me through incident after incident and assuring me that it was not luck, it was not magic, but it was His grace and mercy. It took many years for me to truly put the pieces of the puzzle together but now I fully understand that I was afflicted for a reason. I can truly give God the praise, the honor and the glory. I like the words of this song, "If it had not been for the Lord on my side, where would I be, tell me where would I be?"

Jot down a time when God intervened on your behalf.
What were you feeling at the time?

_____

_____

_____

_____

_____

_____

_____

_____

_____

_____

_____

_____

_____

_____

_____

_____

_____

_____

_____

_____

_____

_____

_____

_____

_____

_____

_____

_____

Psalm 119:71
It is good for me that I have been afflicted;
that I might learn thy statutes.

<u>O – Oppression</u>

According to Wikipedia the definition of oppression is the exercising of authority or power in a burdensome, cruel, or unjust manner.

Many women are living in oppression due to their culture while others are secretly living an oppressed life, fearing what society would say if it was revealed. Their fear will not allow them to speak up and speak out about the abuse.

Having been married to an x-army officer and a martial arts expert, I became accustomed to him making all the decisions in the family. I am originally from Jamaica and we had a decent lifestyle before migrating to the United States. The abuse was heavily masked but my family had their suspicions. However, I never confirmed it. I was working at the bank at the time and my 3 month old and 3 year old sons were being taken care of by the helpers. One day as I returned from lunch I received a call from my husband telling me that we would be migrating to the United States. I was livid. How could he make such a major decision on his own? Then he quickly reminded me that in this family he makes all the decisions and I didn't have a say.

His behavior confirmed that I got into this relationship without getting the green light from God. However, at the time I was convinced that I could fix him and make him into the husband who would respect me and make me happy. Wrong!   If we were to be more patient and let God do His work, we would have less heart aches, less abuse and a more fulfilled life.

Too many of us have experienced some type of oppression in our lives, where we were dictated to and controlled, leaving us with a feeling of helplessness. What a vulnerable place to be.

Sometimes the oppressed victim is reduced to feeling less than dirt, leaving her with a desire to crawl under a rock and hide. It is imperative that you understand that no matter what has happened in your life, God can put you back together and make you whole. God can pull you out from under that rock and bring you to a safe place.

Write about a time in your life when you felt oppressed and hopeless.

_____

_____

_____

_____

_____

_____

_____

_____

_____

_____

_____

_____

_____

_____

_____

_____

_____

_____

_____

_____

Psalm 10:17-18
Lord, you know the hopes of the helpless. Surely you will listen to their cries and comfort them. You will bring justice to the orphans and the oppressed, so people can no longer terrify them."

M – Mental Abuse

According to Wikipedia the definition of Mental Abuse is a form of abuse characterized by a person subjecting or exposing another to behavior that may result in psychological trauma, including anxiety, chronic depression, or post-traumatic stress disorder. Mental abuse will let you admit to things you never did. Such abuse is often associated with situations of power imbalance, such as abusive relationships, bullying, child abuse and abuse in the workplace.

Mental abuse is the one that leaves invisible scars, you see when a victim is mentally abused often times they are reluctant to share it with someone, fearing that they might not believe, seeing there is no evidence. Therefore, many victims live a life of misery and depression, while others end up in a mental institution, leaving a small percent of us who became Free, because of God's Mercy and Grace.

I remember while living in New York, I was accused of having a relationship with one of my customer's at the bank. I remember when I went home that evening I was interrogated from 6:00 p.m. to 6:00 a.m. I did not have to wake up for work because I was already up.

My brain was so fried that after twelve hours of rigid cross questioning and interrogation, I admitted to everything. I admitted to going to lunch, to a hotel and to bed with my customer. I admitted to things I never did!

Jot down a time when you experienced Mental Abuse, What triggered it?

_____

_____

_____

_____

_____

_____

_____

_____

_____

_____

_____

_____

_____

_____

_____

_____

_____

_____

_____

_____

_____

_____

_____

_____

_____

Psalm 27:12
"For they accuse me of things I've never
done and breathe out violence against me."

2 Timothy 1:7
For God hath not given us the spirit of fear; but of power,
and of love, and of a sound mind.

E – Economic Abuse

According to Wikipedia the definition of Economic Abuse is when the abuser has control over the victim's money and other economic resources. In its extreme (and usual) form, this involves putting the victim on a strict "allowance," withholding money at will and forcing the victim to beg for the money until the abuser gives them some money. It is common for the victim to receive less money as the abuse continues.

I was married for fourteen years to a man who agreed for me to go out to work when his commissions were not adequate to take care of the expenses. However, once I started to out-earn him I was forced to quit. Two letters of resignation were written for me.

Having fathered six children there was never enough money to meet the financial needs of our family, yet monies were made available to sustain several extra-marital relationships, while we experienced lack at home.

I have come to the realization that when we re-prioritize our lives and put God first He becomes our source. Not the husband or the children, but God Almighty will see to it that our needs are met.

Was there ever a time when you encountered Economic Abuse, if so how did you cope with it?

_____

_____

_____

_____

_____

_____

_____

_____

_____

_____

_____

_____

_____

_____

_____

_____

_____

_____

_____

_____

_____

_____

_____

_____

_____

_____

_____

Philippians 4:19
But my God shall supply all your needs according to His riches in glory by Christ Jesus.

S – Statistics

According to Wikipedia the definition of Statistics is the study of the collection, organization, analysis, and interpretation of data. It deals with all aspects of this, including the planning of data collection in terms of the design of surveys and experiments.

About 2 - 4 million American women are battered each year by their partners.
Every 9 seconds a woman is battered in the United States.
Every 6 hours a woman is killed by a husband or boyfriend.
40% of women who die are victims of Domestic Violence.
95% of the victims are female.
95-98% of the perpetrators are male.
Battering is the largest single major cause of injury to women.
Women are at a 75% greater risk of being killed after they leave their partners.
About 1/3 of female homicide victims are killed by their partners.
Boys who have witnessed abuse of their mothers are twice as likely to abuse their female partners and children as adults.
Children who witness domestic violence are more likely to commit sexual assault crimes.
Between 3 and 10 million American children witness domestic violence each year.
Children of abused mothers are more likely to attempt suicide, abuse drugs and alcohol, run away from home, and engage in teenage prostitution.
In a 1992 study, 63% of imprisoned kids between ages 11 – 20 were doing time for killing their mother's batterer.

These are the facts, but when you have a relationship with God, you don't have to embrace these negative statistics. God can set you separate and apart from these numbers and let you shine, despite the facts.

While I was raising my children I vowed that we would never become a negative statistic and with the help of God, we did not.

Which of these statistics can you relate to?

_____

_____

_____

_____

_____

_____

_____

_____

_____

_____

_____

_____

_____

_____

_____

_____

_____

_____

_____

_____

_____

_____

_____

_____

Joshua 1:9
Be strong and courageous. Do not be frightened, and do not be dismayed,
for the Lord your God is with you wherever you go.

T – Threats

According to Wikipedia, the definition of a threat is the crime of intentionally or knowingly putting another person in fear of imminent bodily injury. Threat of harm generally involves a perception of injury...physical or mental damage...act or instance of injury, or a material and detriment or loss to a person. A terroristic threat is a crime generally involving a threat to commit violence communicated with the intent to terrorize another.

A word of advice about threats, even if you have received 100 empty threats, never take it lightly. Someone who constantly makes threats is considered an unstable individual, so you never know when they might carry out one of them.

l remember when I was forced to migrate to the United States and I was reluctant to go along with the plan, I was threatened that if I didn't comply, I would never see my boys again.

Then there was another incident that took place in Miami at my brother's house and there was a scene where my husband was aggressively twisting my arm while threatening to kill me, when he moved towards me with blood-shot eyes, God amplified my voice and I screamed so loud that the neighbors called the cops. As we heard the sirens approaching, he made his threat known. "If you ever tell the cops what has been happening I promise your brother will be deported in 24 hours."

You see at that time, I needed my brother, I had torn down the walls of secrecy and confided in him and told him what we were going through. He became my support base, and I could not lose him. He was also here to make a better life for his family and I didn't want to be the one to interfere with that. My brother was a chef and he always showed up at the door with tasty meals and some days when he stopped by, we were very grateful because we literally had no food in the house.

Have you ever been threatened by a partner or, someone close to you?

_____
_____
_____
_____
_____
_____
_____
_____
_____
_____
_____
_____
_____
_____
_____
_____
_____
_____
_____
_____
_____
_____
_____
_____
_____
_____

Psalm 10:7
"Their mouths are full of cursing, lies, and threats.
Trouble and evil are on the tips of their tongues."

Psalm 54:7
For he has delivered me from every trouble, and my eye has looked
in triumph on my enemies.

I – Isolation

Within Domestic Violence, Isolation is commonly used by the perpetrator to remove the victim from her support base and take her to a foreign place where she does not have easy access to her loved ones and becomes solely dependent on the abuser.

My husband completely isolated me from my family, because he was jealous of the bond that we shared. He decided to relocate to the United States so I could not see my family anymore. This caused me to rely solely on him, despite the abuse I had to endure.

It is not uncommon for the victim to unintentionally isolate him or herself during a period of abuse. Often times, young children are neglected by a parent who really cares about them, but in an effort to hide their abuse they isolate themselves. Innocent children can be exposed to harm and danger while an abused parent remains in isolation for an extended period.

If you ever find yourself in a situation where you are isolated, try to always have access to a telephone. Ask God for wisdom and courage and call for help. Anyone living in an abusive relationship should create a 'secret code,' and share with a few individuals who loves you and who you trust. Whenever that code is used they will immediately know that you are in danger and will immediately call for help. Remember when you are shut-in and feeling lonely and dejected, God is always there with you, He is capable of providing a way of escape and getting you out of isolation.

Have you experienced Isolation?

_____

_____

_____

_____

_____

_____

_____

_____

_____

_____

_____

_____

_____

_____

_____

_____

_____

_____

_____

_____

_____

_____

_____

_____

_____

_____

_____

_____

Psalms 142:4
"Look to my right and see; no one is concerned for me.
I have no refuge; no one cares for my life."

Psalms 30:5
For his anger is but for a moment, and his favor is for a lifetime.
Weeping may tarry for the night, but joy comes in the morning.

C – Child abuse

According to Wikipedia the definition of Child Abuse is the physical, sexual, emotional mistreatment, or neglect of a child. In the United States, the Centers for Disease Control and Prevention (CDC) and the Department of Children and Families (DCF) define child maltreatment as any act or series of acts of commission or omission by a parent or other caregiver that results in harm, potential for harm, or threat of harm to a child. Child abuse can occur in a child's home, or in the organizations, schools or communities the child interacts with.

There are four major categories of child abuse: neglect, physical abuse, psychological/emotional abuse, and child sexual abuse
There are over 3 million reports of child abuse and neglect every year in the United States; however, those reports can include multiple children. In 2007, approximately 5.8 million children were involved in an estimated 3.2 million child abuse reports and allegations.

Child abuse is linked to Domestic Violence. Every day, 4 children die from Child Abuse, of which 80% are under 5 years old.

Those are some frightening facts. My son who is now 32 years old, used to say when he was a kid, that you should have a license before you become a parent. It is unfortunate that so many who are having children are not deemed as responsible individuals. Innocent children, who did not ask to be here, end up suffering in the long run.

You cannot be responsible for every child, but do your part to ensure that the children around you are safe. God is very serious about His love and compassion towards little children and we should be also. If you know someone who is causing harm to a little child please report it or bring the matter to an adult who is not afraid to expose the crime. The Child Abuse Hotline # is: 1-800-4-A-Child.

What steps will you take to ensure the safety of the children around you?

_____

_____

_____

_____

_____

_____

_____

_____

_____

_____

_____

_____

_____

_____

_____

_____

_____

_____

_____

_____

_____

_____

_____

_____

_____

Luke 17:2
It is better for a millstone to hang around his neck, and cast into the sea, than to offend one of these little ones.

Mark 10:14
Let the little children come to me and do not hinder them, for the Kingdom of God belongs to such as these.

V – Verbal Abuse

According to Wikipedia, Verbal Abuse also known as reviling or bullying, is best described as an ongoing emotional environment organized by the abuser for the purposes of control. The underlying factor in the dynamic of verbal abuse is the abuser's low regard for him or herself. As a result, the abuser attempts to place their victim in a position to believe similar things about him or herself, a form of warped projection.

Typically, verbal abuse increases in intensity over time and often escalates into physical abuse as well. After exposure to verbal abuse, victims may fall into clinical depression and/ or post-traumatic stress disorder.

Despite being the most common form of abuse, verbal abuse is generally not taken as seriously as other types of abuse, because there is no visible proof. In reality, however, verbal abuse can be more detrimental to a person's health than physical abuse. If started at a young age, verbal abuse contributes to codependency, borderline personality disorder, narcissistic personality disorder, and other psychological disorders that often plague many people into adulthood.

People who feel they are being attacked by a verbal abuser on a regular basis should seek professional counsel and remove themselves from the negative environment whenever possible. Staying with a verbal abuser is damaging for a person's overall well-being; and all steps to change the situation should be pursued.

Verbal abuse includes the following: discounting, mockery, accusing and blaming, judging and criticizing, trivializing, undermining, threatening, name-calling, ordering, sarcasm, denial of anger or abuse, and abusive anger.

Please do not make excuses for verbal abuse; it opens the door for various types of abuse.

From a Believer's perspective; if you ever encounter verbal abuse again, look the abuser in the eyes and say; "No weapon that is formed against me shall prosper; and every tongue *that* shall rise against me in judgment God will condemn."   Isaiah 54:17

Most people have experienced some form of Verbal Abuse at some time or other, do you recall a time when you were Verbally Abused?

_____
_____
_____
_____
_____
_____
_____
_____
_____
_____
_____
_____
_____
_____
_____
_____
_____
_____
_____
_____

_____

Matthew 15:18-20
"But evil words come from an evil heart and defile the person who says them."

I – Ignoring the Warning Signs

Most folks ignore the first warning sign which is verbal abuse, feeling confident that they can change the person. But only God can change the heart of an abuser.

When I was eighteen years old I went to one of my friend's 18th birthday party, with the man who later became my husband. This was only our 2nd date, therefore we were not yet in a committed relationship.

While he was gone to get us drinks, my friend's fourteen year old brother walked up to me and admired the cross-pendant I was wearing. He moved his hand towards the pendant and took a closer look at it. My date walked up just in time to see the kid remove his hand from the pendant.

"Look I know that little boy is trying a thing with you and it is very obvious that you are encouraging him. I was just in time to see him removing his hand from your breast, and you did nothing to stop him. I will kill him; I promise I will kill him. On the other hand what kind of woman are you to just stand there and enjoy it. I'll never give you the opportunity to two-time me again, I will kill you before I let that happen," he responded.

I was humiliated by his harsh and demeaning words; I became a nervous wreck and was shaking beyond control. As he drove me home he apologized emphatically, blaming his out-burst on his abusive upbringing. He swore before God that he would never use an unkind word to me ever again and he would give me the respect I deserved. Unfortunately, I believed him. I dismissed the incident and made a commitment to nurture and mold him into the man I knew he could be.

I wasn't sure if God had him on his priority list, so I took over and decided to give God a hand, I totally ignored the warning signs, and thought I could fix him.

Be honest and jot down at least one time when you ignored a warning sign

_____

_____

_____

_____

_____

_____

_____

_____

_____

_____

_____

_____

_____

_____

_____

_____

_____

_____

_____

_____

_____

_____

_____

_____

_____

_____

_____

Ezekiel 11:19
And I will give them one heart, and I will put a new spirit within you; and I will take the stony heart out of their flesh, and will give them a heart of flesh...

Psalm 55:20-21
"As for this friend of mine, he betrayed me; he broke his promises. His words are as smooth as cream, but in his heart is war. His words are as soothing as lotion, but underneath are daggers!

O – Outlet

The goal of this guide is to encourage you to speak up and speak out against domestic violence. Everyone needs an outlet where they can voice their thoughts and concerns.

If you have been in an abusive relationship for years and like me you have successfully masked it, remember your family and friends might not know, but God does. Begin your healing process by using this guide as a confidant, and then I encourage you to bring the dialogue before the Lord and ask Him to lead you to someone in whom you can confide. In the book of Deuteronomy it reminds us that one can chase a thousand, but two ten thousand. Therefore, there is power in numbers.

Ask God to bring a Ruth or Naomi in your life so you can build a relationship with someone you can trust.

The words of Ruth depict what a relationship with two women of God should look like.

Use this guide to start your healing process…
As you empty the pain of your (past/present) on these pages
Let God direct you to someone you can trust.

_____
_____
_____
_____
_____
_____
_____
_____
_____
_____
_____
_____
_____
_____
_____
_____
_____
_____
_____
_____
_____
_____
_____
_____
_____
_____

Ruth 1: 16-17
But Ruth replied, "Don't urge me to leave you or to turn back from you. Where you go I will go, and where you stay I will stay. Your people will be my people and your God my God. Where you die I will die, and there I will be buried. May the LORD deal with me, be it ever so severely, if anything but death separates you and me."

L – Listen to your loved-ones
How many of us have, or had a 'Praying Mother?'

I can attest to the fact that my mother was usually right and she never stopped praying even though I did not heed her warning. Actually, God showed up many times for me because of my mother's prayers.

Remember that incident in New York, where I was interrogated for twelve hours straight? As I walked to the subway that morning, my brain was in shambles and I cried out to God asking him to get a message to my mother and let her know I was desperately in need of prayers.

You see folks my mother lived in rural Jamaica and I was in Brooklyn New York, but the angels of God delivered the message to her instantly, not having access to phone or internet. My mother cried out to God that day and asked that He would deliver me and my children from the hands of my husband.

Not knowing what was in store that evening when I returned from work I was eager to get an early night's rest because I was drained. But that was not so, the abuse intensified and my husband came very close to stabbing me in the kitchen. However, his plan failed when his cousin suddenly appeared at the nick of time.

You see up to that point I thought I was lucky, until my family called from Jamaica that evening to inform me that Mama had a bike-rider carry a letter to them in Kingston and she asked that they call to let me know that God impressed it on her heart to pray for our safety THAT day and to let me know that God has heard her prayer.

I could not respond to the phone call, because I just cried and cried when I think about the awesomeness of God and that he cared for me and my children, even though I was not 100% committed to Him.

Folks listen to your loved-ones, as they will timely evaluate your prospective fiancés while you are busy trying to deal with the butterflies in your tummy. Many women commit to relationships solely on emotions.

Can you jot down one thing you wished you listened to your family about?

_____

_____

_____

_____

_____

_____

_____

_____

_____

_____

_____

Proverbs 22:24
"Do not associate with a man given to anger; or go with a hot-tempered man lest you learn his ways and become like him."

2 Timothy 3:1-5
"They will be boastful and proud, scoffing at God . . . and ungrateful. They will consider nothing sacred. They will be unloving and unforgiving; they will slander others and have no self-control; they will be cruel and have no interest in what is good. They will betray their friends, be reckless, be puffed up with pride, and love pleasure rather than God. They will act as if they are religious but they will reject the power that could make them godly. You must stay away from people like that."

E – Envision Change

If you truly believe the verse in Proverbs that states: 'As a man thinks in his heart so is he,' you would spend more time thinking Godly thoughts, positive thoughts, uplifting thoughts, thoughts that will bring you to a place in God where you have never been before.

If you are dealing with Domestic Violence and you feel unsafe, ask God to provide a way of escape and take the necessary steps to be safe.

FORGIVE your abuser and move on. (Unforgiveness will block your blessings).

Envision yourself Free! Free to serve God without hindrances, free to be a stable parent to your children. It is believed that a child is better off with one responsible, God fearing parent, than to be with both parents where domestic violence is present.

Promise me that from this day on, you will speak Life to your situation, Life to yourself, and Life to your children.

Life and Death are in the power of the tongue, so speak Life, never death..

Live your life as though you would want your kids to mirror what they see in you.

Think about your current relationship,
What would you like to see change?

_____
_____
_____
_____
_____
_____
_____
_____
_____
_____
_____
_____
_____
_____
_____
_____
_____
_____
_____
_____
_____
_____
_____
_____
_____
_____
_____
_____
_____

Proverbs 23:7
As a man thinks in his heart, so is he....

N – Never Lose Faith

No matter how dark or hopeless you feel your situation is remember that God can do all things, and you can do all things through God who strengthens you. Therefore never lose faith, and know that things WILL get better.

When I think of a woman in the bible who never lost faith, I think of Hannah.   Peninnah and Hannah were married to Elkanah. Peninnah had children and Hannah had none. Each year when they went up to the altar to offer sacrifices unto the Lord, Peninnah took pride in teasing Hannah and reminding her that she could not have children. Well this went on for years and this particular year, Hannah became really upset, she began to cry and would not eat. She cried out to God and that evening she made her way to the house of the Lord. Hannah cried as she prayed to God, despite her barrenness, God opened up her womb and she conceived and gave birth to Samuel.

I believe there is power when a woman cries out to God, I think it touches God's heart and He responds. It has happened in my life countless times.

What areas in your life do you need to exercise faith?
What steps will you take to strengthen your faith?

_____

_____

_____

_____

_____

_____

_____

_____

_____

_____

_____

_____

_____

_____

_____

_____

_____

_____

_____

_____

_____

_____

_____

_____

_____

_____

_____

_____

_____

Hebrews 11:6
And without faith it is impossible to please God, because anyone
who comes to him must believe that he exists and that he rewards
those who earnestly seek Him.

Cast All your Cares Upon Him Because He Cares For You (1 Peter 5:7).

You might ask, "What does this verse have to do with Domestic Violence?"

Everything!

Whether you're being used, abused or rejected---Cast it on the Lord! But it doesn't stop there, it says ALL---

So whatever else you might be holding on to, cast them All on Him.

It is said that; Worry, Stress and Depression is the root cause of most illnesses.

Did we not get the memo, that we should cast ALL our worries on Him…

I hope you got it because I did and as a result, my life is far more meaningful today. Glory be to God!

Examine your life and jot down some of the things that's causing you concern, in other words things that you are worrying about...

_____

_____

_____

_____

_____

_____

_____

_____

_____

_____

_____

_____

_____

_____

_____

_____

_____

_____

_____

_____

_____

_____

_____

_____

_____

_____

_____

_____

Matthew 6:31
So do not worry, saying, 'What shall we eat?' or 'What shall we drink?' or 'What shall we wear?'

End the Cycle

Unfortunately many women stay in abusive relationships for months, years, and even a life-time. It is important to end the cycle of abuse and take a step of faith towards your freedom.

In my situation the following event is what finally put an end to the cycle of abuse. That day the house was eerie, as FEAR was dripping from its walls, we were on pins, not being sure what our next move should be. I did not know how much more I could bear, my nerves were shattered and the kids were frightened.

(You'll have to read the whole story from; Crosses To Bear Love To Share).' The build-up that led to the scene that made me end the cycle was traumatizing, but God showed up again for me and Goodness and Mercy had their daggers drawn. So the gun that was held at my temple with my six kids lined up next to me to kill us, one by one, could not go off, because God intervened.

The day my husband left, he looked back at me and my six children, ranging from 3-13 years and said, "Nina you and your six kids get out of my life. They won't amount to anything; they'll all drop out of school and end up on drugs. None of you will ever amount to anything." Well, God blocked that curse and poured out his blessings upon us. Raising six kids singlehandedly without a dime in child support was not easy and today all of them are successful in their respective fields. **But Psalm 23 became my close companion. *THE LORD IS MY SHEPHERD* I SHALL NOT WANT.* THOU PREPAR- EST A TABLE BEFORE ME IN THE PRESENCE OF MINE ENEMIES.* THOU ANOINTEST MY HEAD WITH OIL MY CUP RUNNETH OVER.* SURELY GOODNESS AND MERCY SHALL FOLLOW ME ALL THE DAYS OF MY LIFE AND I WILL DWELL IN THE HOUSE OF THE LORD FOREVER!**

I will serve God for as long as I live! Experience the joy that I have found and renew your commitment to serving the Lord today…

If you are in an abusive relationship, what steps will you take to effect a positive change?

_____

_____

_____

_____

_____

_____

_____

_____

_____

_____

_____

_____

_____

_____

_____

_____

_____

_____

_____

James 2:14-17
What does it profit, my brethren, if someone says he has faith but does not have works? Can faith save him? If a brother or sister is naked and destitute of daily food, and one of you says to them, "Depart in peace, be warmed and filled," but you do not give them the things which are needed for the body, what does it profit? Thus also faith by itself, if it does not have works, is dead.

<u>Warning Signs</u>

Many of the signs women are taught to interpret as caring, attentive, and romantic are actually early warning signs for future abuse. Some examples include:

INTRUSION: Constantly asks you where you are going, who you are with, etc.

ISOLATION: Insists that you spend all or most of your time together, cutting you off from friends and family.

POSSESSION AND JEALOUSY: Accuses you of flirting/having sexual relationships with others; monitors your clothing/make-up.

NEED FOR CONTROL: Displays extreme anger when things do not go his way; attempts to make all of your decisions.

UNKNOWN PASTS / NO RESPECT FOR WOMEN: Secretive about past relationships; refers to women with negative remarks, etc.

No more Running from God, I now Run for God

I am the 11th of 12 children, and of the twelve pregnancies, mine was the most life threatening. From a fetus in the womb the enemy has been trying to take me out, but despite the challenges and with the help of God, I survived!

I was raised in a Christian home by parents who loved Jesus. My father was an Elder in the church and my mother was a Speaker, Teacher, and Prayer Warrior. My sister and I got saved when I was eleven and we got baptized shortly after. I grew up seeing my mother feed the hungry, clothe the naked, pray for the sick and constantly win souls for the Lord. I had much admiration for her but at that time, that lifestyle seemed dull and I wanted some excitement. In order to attend high school, I went to live with my father's niece who I affectionately called, 'Auntie Prim,' but like Mama, she was serious about the things of the Lord. So I put everything on hold and decided that I would wait until after graduation to see what I was really missing in the world.

I met my husband the week prior to graduation so my dreams of exploring the world ended abruptly. After fourteen years of a severely abusive marriage, laced with fear, I was left penniless with six children in a home from which we were being evicted.

Though I loved Jesus, I was not totally committed to serving Him because I became very involved with nurturing my children. Jesus was not my number one priority at the time, and I thought that I could do everything in my own strength as opposed to His.

Raising 6 children without a dime in child support was not easy, but God always made a way for us, moving from food stamp recipient to bank manager. The years went by quickly and before long some of the kids were in college, I owned my own home and embraced a lifestyle change. But I knew in my heart that God was still not my number one priority.

December 2009 I had a hysterectomy and returned home to continue working on one of my titles. Due to the extended hours of sitting at my computer, I developed blood clots in the legs which travelled to both lungs. Six weeks later I was admitted to the hospital with a Pulmonary Embolism. It's a miracle how I am alive today. I was on the oxygen tank for 6 weeks and on blood thinners for 6 months. About the third night after I was discharged from the hospital, I told my son David, to take a break and sleep upstairs as he never left my side during the entire illness. I also started feeling a little better. He was hesitant to leave me but I insisted. He held up his phone and said, "Mom if you need me for anything, please call." About 1:30 a.m. I felt as though someone was trying to choke me to death. I quickly opened my eyes, frightened to think that there was someone in my life who wanted to kill me, but there was no one! I realized then it was a spiritual battle. By this time the shortness of breath returned but only 10 times worse. I called David, but there was no answer. I called my daughter, but no answer. It was as though the enemy was laughing somewhere in the corner of my mind, "I have been trying to take you out forever, but tonight is the night. Tomorrow morning when your kids wake up they will find you dead." I pleaded the blood of Jesus and I cried out the name of Jesus and gave myself a shot in the belly as the breathing narrowed down to almost my last breath. Suddenly, my daughter who is a sound sleeper walked in my room.

God woke up my 3 year old grandson and had him go over to his mother's room and woke her up and told he wanted juice. This had never happened before. My grandson went back to bed and God prompted my daughter to come to my room to check on me. When she saw me her eyes popped open as she had no clue what was going on at the time. My daughter prayed for me and stayed up and made signs of powerful promises from God's word of healing and restoration and posted them around the mirror and on the door. These signs alerted the enemy and his legion of angels that I was off limits and that I shall live and not die, to proclaim the name of the Lord. The blood of Jesus permeated that room and there was no place for Satan.

When my little grandson came in my room the following morning, I was tearful as I hugged him, because I knew how close I came to dying. "Jamesie Boo, do you know that God used you to save Grandma's life last night?" Then he looked at me somewhat puzzled, and then said. "Grandma, I was fast asleep and then someone popped my eyes open, popped my eyes open." Then I thought of Samuel…

Folks my years of running from God is over, I feel like Jonah who did not want to heed the call of God on his life, so what did he do? He ran! I have wasted over 50 precious years having a lukewarm relationship with the Lord. I wish I hadn't, but I thank God I am still young and vibrant to make up for all the wasted years.

You see, my relationship with God was like an insurance policy, and though I would pray every day and read the bible I did not fully commit my life to God. I would take out my policy when I was in dire straits. I would take it out when death was staring me in the face and there was no way out. I would take it out when I was having challenges while being a single parent. I would take it out when people I cared for became ill or died. But when life was going really well and I was prospering, I rarely took it out! Notice that I only cried out to God when I needed Him to do something that only He alone could do. My children might even be surprised to read this, because though I portrayed God, my life did not line up with the principles set out in His word. Today I am thankful for all the battles He has fought to keep me alive and after years of running, today; 'I press on toward the goal to win the prize for which God has called me heavenward in Christ' Jesus Philippians 3:14.

*I revised my first book "Crosses To Bear Love To Share" in 2004 and reprinted it in 2010. I recommitted my life to the Lord in March 2010...

Sister Nina Hart
sixheartspublishing@gmail.com
www.sixheartspublishing.com

A Man with a Repentant Heart

Vernon Roberts was a youth of the 60's and the Civil Rights Movement in Chicago. He married his elementary school sweetheart and became a father and a husband in 1965. As an adolescent, he was taught all of the negative ways to deal with women, which almost always produced violence. Growing up, he saw the physical and mental abuse of women as a way of life.

This violence became a part of his marriage. The misuse and abuse of women was a part of his life. In the late 60's, he ended up living on the streets for over 12 years. He also was incarcerated for two years. Shortly after he got out, he found himself headed to Florida, where he met his present wife.

Pastor Vernon turned his life over to God in 1975. He had to ask God to teach him how to be a man of God and how to treat females. He said God began to talk to him and show him how to treat His daughters. One of Pastor Vernon's favorite scriptures is Ephesians 5:25 "Husbands love your wives, even as Christ loved the Church, and gave Himself for it." God did not create women for men to use and abuse, but for men to appreciate women as a help mate. Not only did God create man but also woman to help man conceive and replenish the earth.

Men have taken the role of women out of proportion, by not doing their part to provide and protect; nourishing and cherishing what God has blessed him with. As years went by, he began seeking the Kingdom of God more and more. He came upon Romans, the 9th chapter where there is the illustration of the potter having the authority over the clay. He realized this is what God has with man; the Divine Authority to mold us, break us down and rebuild us in His image. As he sought the Kingdom, he asked God to mold him like that clay.

One of his most painful memories, but also the point that brought the deep desire to get out of the cycle of abuse was when Vernon went to visit his ex-wife's mother, she asked him, "Why did you disfigure your wife's face, and then go back and lay with her and tell her how much you loved her; how did you feel, looking at her black eye, her busted lip or her swollen face?"

Vernon Roberts wants every man to remember this – when God created females, their lives were placed in our care, and men are supposed to protect – there is a difference between protection and power. The instinct to protect puts our power in check so that we do not hurt. Marriage makes you and your wife one flesh. What you afflict on your spouse you are really afflicting on yourself. Are you demonstrating the love that Christ has for His bride, the Church?

Pastor Vernon Roberts ,
Orlando, Fl
jll_om@yahoo.com
 www.jesusthelightoflife.org

Forgiving my Past to Free My Future

Life will always throw you some curves. However, I had no idea the journey I was about to take at 23 years old would forever change my life and make me the person that I am today. I was a young bride and entertaining in my home for the very first time. We had just finished having a great dinner and I was waiting for the pie to get ready so that we could have it for dessert. The couple we were entertaining were newlyweds as well and ministers of the gospel, as we were. We were having a conversation and I made the mistake of disagreeing with what my husband said, and he jumped up and slapped me. I was embarrassed and shocked. I jumped up and ran out of the house with tears flowing and my heart racing. While running, not knowing where I was going, I tried to process what had just happened to me.

I wasn't raised in a home where I witnessed or heard of any domestic abuse. I had no idea that there was a word for what happened to me until four children and nineteen years later. Yes you are reading correctly I stayed in that marriage for nineteen years. I finally got the courage to leave in the 17th year with the help of my four children. They were the ones who shocked me back into reality after 17 years of my life had passed by. The kids were between the ages of 8 and 12 years old, when they placed themselves between me and their father and told him he wasn't going to hit me again. You see, they had enough, and it was then that I took courage and said if these babies that God gave me to protect, were now protecting me then I needed to do something. I had no idea that statistics shows that 85% of teens kill their abusers. I was not only in danger but I had my children in danger by allowing them to act on my behalf. My then husband was startled and ran in the room and stayed their overnight. The next morning he got up and left the house. I told my kids that I was going to change the locks and when he comes banging and begging don't open it. I promised them I would protect them from then on.

I had no idea that there was a purpose in my pain and that I had the ability to leave that marriage long before I did. The church tells you, until death do you part, however, it never told me to be a sacrificial lamb. Jesus had paid the price for me and I did not need to pay it again. I took my life back. It has been 16 years since the divorce and I have put my four children through college, and they are all living productive lives, and serving in their communities. I've had the opportunity to travel the world and have written 4 books and started a non-profit organization serving domestic abuse called "The Soul of a Woman Foundation."

Don't let anyone take your dreams away or the promise that God has for your life. Who you see in the mirror every day is not all there is; it's just the beginning of something great. I encourage you to choose greatness and learn how to turn your pain into divine power with God who is limitless.

Valorie N. Parker
Businesswoman, Author, Inspirational Speaker
www.fromthesoulofawoman.com

My Faith was Tested….But God Brought me Through

I got married in February 2007 at the age of 22. I was in college at the time doing my associates degree. Two weeks later I became pregnant. I had some health issues and had to drop out of college. After the baby came, I wanted to resume my studies but it was not financially feasible. My husband had made a bad investment and he was taking home approximately 30% less of his salary.

Things worsened and we could barely manage to buy food and take care of the baby. My mother helped with diapers and food for the baby. Over time he got a raise on the job and things began to look-up, but not for long. We began having marital issues and the lying and disrespect started. It was as though I was being haunted, I had no peace, but it got worse, because he joined forces with his new girlfriend and together they made my life miserable, and they still do, even now.

But my relationship with Jesus gave me an inner peace despite the loud noises and the mockery. Financially it got worse and my son's allowance was only a fraction of what he should pay. So I had to put my hopes aside regarding school and find a job to provide for my child.

I put my resume out there. However, many nights I went to bed hungry as I had no money for food and I am not comfortable always asking for help. All I wanted was for God to help me get a job so I could help myself. One day while I was home with the baby there was absolutely nothing inside the house to eat except for a little milk and oats. I sat on the step at my back door and I cried and cried. I remember praying for a miracle then and was inspired to read about the life of Job. He also went through a great ordeal and despite everything he did not give up on God. As I read I saw how God delivered Job from all his troubles and blessed him tenfold. I told myself if God did it for Job, He can do it for me too.

It had gotten to the point where my mother and I could not get along, we got into a real bad fight one evening and she almost killed me. On that very evening I packed my bags, took my son and ran away from home. I was away for two weeks and something inside stirred me to return home. I didn't have any money so I asked a friend for a ride home. I spoke to my mother and asked if we can at least try to get along. A few days later I received a call from my church sister to inform me that there was a vacancy for a junior accountant at the Jamaica Baptist Union and that I should email my resume to her by the following morning.

She didn't know that I didn't have a dime to my name, didn't have a computer, didn't have a car, didn't have money for the internet café, so many more things I didn't have, but I had Jesus.

It was one challenge after another, but I refused to lose focus and dilute my efforts in securing this job. The first interview went well and I was called back for a second interview scheduled in the city and I lived in the country. Money was a huge issue, I charted a taxi and when he informed me of the price, he couldn't help noticing my facial expressions. He asked me what was the occasion and I told him. He said to just give him what I had and not to worry. He gave me his number and asked me to call him when I got the job; it's as if he had more faith than I did. Right after I left the interview, I called the taxi driver and told him that I landed the job. I cried happy tears as I thanked Jesus and the interviewer also.

The taxi driver was really happy for me and it was then that I knew that things were starting to turn around for me, my faith in God was beginning to pay off, ...no more hunger. God is great!

My ex-husband and his girlfriend traumatize my son and I consistently. Right now I don't see a way out, but I know God can make a way where there is no way. I am faced with difficulties every day but I will remain steadfast and faithful to the Lord. I am trusting Him to take my son and I out of the situation we are in. I need to go back to college and complete my degree so I can qualify for a higher pay grade which will help me regain my independence and become financially stable.

But in the meantime, I will continue to trust and have faith in the Lord. He has taken me this far and as long as I don't turn my back on Him, He won't turn his back on me. Our God is a great God. I often tell people, faith is like money...if you go to the market, you can't get food without money and if you go to God for help you can't get it without faith.

This is my testimony and I really hope it will be an inspiration to someone.

Renee Panton, (Jamaica)
reneepanton@yahoo.com

<u>Madness was at my Door</u>

Miguel was tall dark and handsome sweet and very kind and we talked and laughed a lot. We spent a lot of time together and in no time he moved himself into my home. Miguel would have dinner ready when I got home from work and the house would be clean. We had a great relationship or so I thought. He was considerate and very loving but he had a dark side to him that was hidden under the mask that he wore so well. I did not identify the demons that he had within him until it was almost too late.

Miguel was very jealous. At first I was flattered by his jealous remarks. I assured him that he had nothing to worry about but then what was once cute became annoying. If I was not home by exactly 6:30 p.m. then I had to give an account of my whereabouts. Again, I thought, wow this man really cares about me, what I did not understand that this was leading to dangerous grounds. It was not very long into our relationship that I realized that Miguel was a liar; a gambler and he lived off women. I had made a very big mistake becoming involved with this man.

One weekend we had a big argument. I told Miguel he was a con-man he was furious. It seemed like I had touched a nerve. I told him I wanted him out of my life. Quickly I packed an overnight bag and called my sister to tell her I would be spending the weekend with her. When I attempted to leave the house, Miguel blocked the doorway, and unplugged the phones in the house and hid them. I was held captive in my own home for the entire weekend. During that time I was interrogated and followed around the house to make sure I did not escape. I was terrified I was unable to communicate with my family. Monday morning he apologized, he knew I had to go to work and he would have to release me.

My sister called me at work that Monday and asked me what happened to me and why I did not answer the house phone. I was too ashamed to tell her the truth so I hid it from her. My Mother warned me about Miguel and advised me not to get involved. My sister could not stand him, so how could I tell them they were right? My friends at work knew that something was wrong. I was embarrassed and felt stupid for being so naïve.

There were many other incidents, but two still stand out in my mind, I now realize that God truly had his hand on me. One night while in bed we had another argument Miguel tried to suffocate me with a pillow, I struggled and got a breath and screamed and pleaded for my life. The following day, the neighbors told my landlord they heard screams, yet, they never called the police. Miguel apologized again, I was too scared to run. I felt like a trapped mouse.

The second incident Miguel and I quarreled once more then he started to break my beautiful stemware a gift from my parents. When I told him he had no right to break my things, he tried to throw a pot of boiling macaroni he was cooking at the time on me. I ran as quickly as I could to avoid getting burned. Miguel then got a knife and started to plunge it into a new pair of sneakers he had purchased that day, the way he plunged the knife into the shoes I knew that he was possessed and that I was in big trouble. He then proceeded to light a coat on fire in the middle of the kitchen floor. I screamed and tried to run, again he stopped me and I saw madness approaching the doorway of my mind. The constant stress and abuse from the relationship had weakened me; my mind could no longer handle it. I felt that I was on the brink of madness. I could not take it anymore.

There is so much more to this story, but I must stop here. What you need to know is that finally I broke free from this man. I had to take out an order of protection against him. Miguel and I had to go before a judge. I had to leave my home because he told the judge he had no place to live. The judge gave him three weeks to find a place to move to. At the end of the three weeks I reentered my home with a police escort, there was Miguel in the kitchen cooking as if nothing was wrong. The policeman ordered him to leave. I regained my home, but lost so much. I was shattered, I was ashamed, I was depressed, BUT I was finally free of this monster.

I praise God, that he remembered me even though I was in depths of sin. I praise God because he loved me so much and allowed me to live and repent and he had given me the opportunity to tell my story, and I know that God allowed me to go through this because he knew that someone else needed to hear it. I pray that if it is you that you will take heed and not make the same mistakes. I pray that you will consult the Holy Spirit before you enter into covenant with someone. God will always direct our path if we allow him to.

Ingrid E. Campbell
Contact information
eldercampbell@gmail.com
754-235-1039

<u>Forgiveness after Adultery</u>

It all began during the years 1980 – 1991 when Ricky and I dated at a very young age, I was only 15 years old and he was 17. We started out as friends and later became high school sweethearts. We were both innocent about a lot of things pertaining to relationships, but I was more outgoing and dated throughout our relationship. After all, I was very young and still at the prime of my life. Therefore, I did not take our relationship as serious as Ricky did. I thought I was God's gift to men, very arrogant and kept up with myself very well. Ricky saw me as his dream girl but the feeling was not mutual.

We continued dating until we eventually got married, I was only 19 years old and he was 21. Ricky enlisted in the military and it required us relocating to California, where our first daughter Sasha was born. We were doing well financially and we loved living in Monterey, California. While there, I finished my Associates degree at Monterey Peninsula College, while Ricky travelled extensively in the Army.

The years went by quickly and after four years Ricky decided not to re-enlist, he wanted to resign from the Army and return to living in Miami, Florida because he missed his family and friends.

Ricky began to hang out with other friends and I started to hang out also and would party extensively. However, we made time for church, though our hearts were not in line with the word of God. We truly loved the Lord but we didn't want to miss out on the pleasures of the world either, so we were serving both masters.

By this time we had our second daughter, Natasha. Ricky had stopped going to church and I was left to take my girls without their father, but based on how I was raised I was determined to take my children to church regardless of what was happening.

God was always with me as many times I escaped His judgment. In 1996 my husband started hanging with the wrong crowd and he became a leader of a motorcycle crew, which led him to becoming promiscuous. He began to ignore me and began looking intently at other women. One thing led to another. Ricky started to date lots of young pretty girls during our marriage, of course, at this time for me, neglect was inevitable. Ricky continued on this journey of adultery for several years with different young women, until he met one specific young lady who captured his heart. She became a hindrance in our marriage. He began to date her and had an adulterous relationship with this woman for 6-7 years while he was still married to me. I lived with it in misery and embarrassment and I would cringe when I thought about what people might be saying. Obviously at that time she did not care, as she was bound by Satan. My life became a total mess. Our children cried relentlessly as my husband slept away from home many nights.

Ricky began to ignore the children by being busy with his friends, he would leave the house with dozens of friends who were a part of his bike crew. Weekend after weekend they would meet up with different girls on their motorcycles, there were over 50 riders, most of them were in adulterous relationships. Ricky was the one leading the crew to hell. This particular young lady became attached in such a way, she became a soul tie. She became pregnant with a child for my husband. This was one of the most devastating times of my life; I would not wish this on my worst enemy. I became very angry and bitter. It led me to a place of wanting to take matters in my own hands. I began to stalk both Ricky and his mistress. It led me to holding my husband Ricky at gun point while I followed him to her house. So much fighting and fussing I became very weary and was not able to finish nursing school. I began to wish him dead; the pain was so terrible. I was on an emotional rollercoaster, always looking through the window along with my two daughters wondering when my husband would come home. Like most men, he did not want to move out, as he'd want to have his cake and eat it too!

I always prayed and continued to attend church and school on a regular basis, even while I partied. I would go places and see my husband Ricky all over with this young girl and then he would leave as he was forewarned by his friends that I was coming to the night club where he was. Then he became angry and left with her. Anyway, the disrespect continued for years, until she became pregnant at which time I became angrier. I continued to wish that he was dead, just to get him off the face of the earth so the pain would go away, but it continued. It so happened that they both became frustrated with each other, when they were faced with the responsibilities of raising a child. The fun was over! The new born baby needed tender love and care.

I was still very bitter and I began to argue that the child was not his. I began to tell him to leave and move on, but Ricky did not leave. God had a plan and God takes the foolish things to confound the wise. What I thought was devastating God knew I could handle it. God turned what the devil planned for evil around for good. Soon after, God used my brother's death as a sacrifice to draw not only my husband but many others to Christ and gave me the strength to get through one of my most trying times in my life. This young lady was also drawn along with her family to Christ. We all became friends and started to attend the same church where we all are saved and sanctified. Ricky and I became Pastors in the church. The little girl who is now a teenager comes and spends time with us as a family. In the midst of all this, I was able to finish my Bachelors in Health Service Administration and my Masters Degree in Management. My Husband and I have a Ministry in the Auto Industry where we help God's people get from under the bondage of 'Car Loans,' and help them own a car that's fully paid for, from the auto-auction.

Over the years we have had hundreds of satisfied customers that we have put in luxury cars and others, in economical cars. Pastor Ricky delivers everything in style, but the customer is most thrilled because there are no car payments.

Today we are a force to reckon with, we are on the battle field for the Lord. The Lord has called me to lead a prayer line for women and Pastor Ricky, a prayer line for men. Who else could have done this but Jesus? Today Pastor Ricky and I have fallen in love all over again, but more importantly, we've both fallen in love with Jesus. "We overcame by the blood of the lamb and the word of our testimony." Through God there is forgiveness after adultery. However, each case is different and only God knows your situation. Married couples have to love and respect each other, and stay committed to each other, despite the temptation. However, it is hard to achieve this in your own flesh, because the flesh is weak. My advice to you is no matter what your situation is turn it over to the Lord, acknowledge Him in ALL that you do, and He will direct your path.

Pastor Elaine Bookal:
email: lovegod85@hotmail.com

<u>Heart of God</u>

I grew up in a home where domestic violence was present, from the age of nine, I saw my father beat my mother and I remember telling her that I would never get married or allow that to happen to me. I hated men so much that I was serious about never getting married until I met my ex-husband. We met when I was only thirteen so he had a lot of time to convince me that he would never hurt me. I had no reason not to believe him. We grew so close that everyone thought we would be together forever and on August 23, 2003 it became official.

At that time my husband was enlisted in the Jamaican Army and about three days after our wedding he was sent to England where he served for one year. Though we were practically together for six years, now that I had become his wife, I wanted us to spend more time together, so I was not excited about the decision for him to leave. Every day I woke up I looked forward to my husband returning home and before long the year swiftly went by, the day finally came and…the man that returned was a totally different person from the man that I hugged with teary eyes and said good-bye to twelve months prior.He was a complete stranger! That day the calls started coming in and I became insecure and nervous.

I became pregnant with my beautiful daughter but that did not stop the blatant disrespect. Calls after calls came in from different women along with pictures I found with his belongings. Sometimes I felt like leaving and then the reality hit me that I was pregnant and I needed to stay in the marriage. At the time my husband was not working in the town we were living in, so that posed a challenge as far as the amount of time we spent together. One evening he came home and assured me that he wanted to be in his daughter's life and that we needed to make the move together as a family. In spite of doubts about his sincerity I decided to go along with the plan. It was not long before his true colors surfaced. I journeyed down a very dark path because the man I fell in love with was no longer caring and respectful. I was actually afraid of him. My self esteem was stripped away but with the help of God I gave birth to my little angel.

I started to gain weight and that made it worst, I felt unattractive; big, ugly, and disgusting. I was told that I would never amount to anything and when I asked him to help me go back to school he told me he would never help me because he did not want me to get a higher level of education and later kick him to the curb. This man described me in the most degrading way. I often felt like my soul had died.

One night I got the scare of my life and that is what gave me the strength to leave him. He came home one night after he was out drinking with his friends and started to fight me. He hit me and put his hands around my neck, being trained in the army, he knew the pressure points. I tried to escape and when I finally did I ran to the kitchen and picked up a knife. I thought that he would back off but that made him even angrier and he moved towards me with vengeance. As he came at me, my baby got up and started to cry and immediately I pictured my daughter on the news, as though she had been hurt, so I dropped the knife and he caught it and swung it after my stomach. I put my hand in the way to protect my stomach and today I have a scar on my hand that will be with me for the rest of my life. It was the prayers of my mother, the love of my family and friends, and more so, it was the grace of God that spared my life. Folks it all started with the verbal abuse. It broke me down in ways that took away my desire to live. When I looked in the mirror, I only saw an empty shell, no soul, no heart, no mind, nothing, just emptiness.

Today thank God I am still standing, a single parent to my daughter and a survivor of domestic violence. If you are in a situation like this you can make it, just get help and let God be your guide.

Averie Bradley, Florida, Avrie26@comcast.net

Battered but not Shattered

Living a life of façade, lies, hypocrisy, hurting while worshipping, praising, preaching, teaching, evangelizing around the country, going into churches, laughing, yet still my heart was tearing apart.

After several years of unfaithful, abusive marriage, the Lord Himself spoke to me and told me; "Be ye separated from among them."

I could not understand why the Lord was telling me this and not knowing or understanding what God was telling me, but I finally got it; My husband was going to kill me if I didn't leave him.

I concur with the scripture; "The Lord giveth and the Lord taketh."

Often times my abuser would be sleeping around with other women which caused me to go to the doctor every month for infections etc. I was being so stressed that I felt I was on the verge of a nervous breakdown.

I was on 'valium' medication to calm my nerves but I didn't want to become dependent on this drug.

Believe it or not, both of us were in church every Sunday, laughing with everyone and praying as if everything was fine...

What hypocrisy?

But I thank God because He knew my breaking point and I decided to walk out of the marriage, as a matter of fact, I ran.

The Lord delivered me and saved me from a marriage that almost killed and aborted my Purpose. My husband was a monster, a pervert, a womanizer, who slept with all othe helpers. I had to run for my life...

After moving out of the matrimonial home, I found peace. The Lord anointed me afresh and told me there is purpose in me and He holds my future in His hands.

I decided to go to bible school and pursued my bachelors degree in theology. I went further and did Pastoral Counseling and received my masters degree.

After several years of a broken marriage and separation I decided to give up the marriage totally by filing for divorce.

I am now a servant of the Most High God, separated, set apart, for the glory of God, I am His mouth piece, in and out of season.

I challenge you women who are in abusive marriages, know your Purpose, know who you are in Christ Jesus.Know when God is saying, 'Walk.'

Separate yourself because His glory cannot shine through you if every day you are in confusion and turmoil, He will not dwell where there is confusion and fuss.He wants us to be healthy and be in peace, to hear from Him and do His will..

Do not let anyone abort your Purpose.
God has a plan for you, don't quit, the devil is a liar...

I am now an ordained Minister, preaching and teaching the word of God as I walk daily in my Purpose.

My ex-husband remarried, living in agony with the woman he left me for, never the less I forgave him. We both are able to laugh and talk now.

It is good to forgive and be released.

People who hurt you will turn around and even bless you and speak well about you.

I have seen my ex-husband come around and was sorry for all he did to me.

I am now living a victorious life in Christ Jesus, fully committed, single for such a time, enjoying God's purpose for my life daily, as I daily do His will.

Remember, know your purpose and God's will for your life and never let the devil kill your purpose.

I am a Promise, I am a Possibility, with a great big bundle of Potentially… I am learning daily to do God's Will, be humble but most of all be 'Holy!'

Rev. Beverley Robinson, BA, MA.
bevvyrob@yahoo.com

Important Telephone Numbers

National Domestic Violence Hotline: 800-799-7233

Safe Horizon's Domestic Violence Hotline: 800.621.HOPE

Child Abuse Hotline: 1-800-4-A-Child

Suicide Hotline: 1-800-SUICIDE or

                                               800-784-2433

Office of Victims of Crimes: 202-307-5983

Safe Horizon's Crime Victims Hotline: 866.689.HELP

Safe Horizon's Rape, Sexual Assault

& Incest Hotline: 212.227.3000

Legal Shield: 305-303-1002

Telephone to Glory

Jeremiah 33:3
'Call to me and I will answer you and tell you great and
unsearchable things you do not know.'

<u>Freedom</u>

Free me so I can spread my wings and fly to a place where I'll be finally safe

Rest is what I need, what would I give for just one night of peaceful sleep?

Eyes that are weary, eyes that have cried, eyes that are looking into a future that's bright.

Ears that have listened to the noise and the screams, the abuse and the cursing, hoping it's only a dream.

Desire is a passionate feeling deep from within, slowly erasing the pain of the past and a new life to begin…

Only God alone knows the level of pain I've endured, His promises are true and one day I'll be fully restored

My life is nothing short of a miracle and the fact that I'm still alive reminds me that I must let go and let God by listening to the voice inside...

Nina Hart

Additional Notes

_____

_____

_____

_____

_____

_____

_____

_____

_____

_____

_____

_____

_____

_____

_____

_____

_____

_____

_____

_____

_____

_____

_____

_____

_____

_____

_____

_____

_____

_____

_____

_____

_____

_____

_____

_____

_____

_____
_____
_____
_____
_____
_____
_____
_____
_____
_____
_____
_____
_____
_____
_____

Miss Hart speaks globally on the topic of domestic violence.
She also conducts workshops and seminars.

For more information please visit www.ninahart.org
or write to her at nina@ninahart.org

www.ingramcontent.com/pod-product-compliance
Lightning Source LLC
Chambersburg PA
CBHW071019040426

42443CB00007B/859